P9-ARC-055

The Buffy-Porson

The Buffy-Porson

A CAR YOU CAN BUILD AND DRIVE

by Peter and Mike Stevenson

CHARLES SCRIBNER'S SONS / NEW YORK

Contents

For Uncle Bill....

Who else?

1 3 5 7 9 11 13 15 17 19 RD/C
20 18 16 14 12 10 8 6 4 2

Printed in the
United States of America
Library of Congress
Catalog Card Number 73-1363
SBN 684-13436-5 (cloth)

One
Getting
Started

This is the story of the Buffy-Porson (a small racer of great spirit) and how it grew—from a pile of dusty lumber into the sporting machine we see above.

It's the story of how a fellow (much like the fellow seen on these pages risking the "dreaded sideslip") can build himself a Buffy-Porson for his own use, with just a little help from an older friend. It's also the story of how a number of young sportsmen (and women) can use a Buffy-Porson to pass many a golden afternoon in the glorious, exhausting sport of "Downhill Racing." For, it seems, you can get just as much sport coming down a hill in a well-built coaster as you can in an Olympic bobsled race, or in the giant slalom.

Don't let anybody kid you; building a car to drive (even a coaster) is a big project. And it takes the kind of person who can stick with a job to build a Buffy-Porson (but then, maybe that's what separates the Buffy-Porson drivers from those who run along behind).

All you need to start a downhill race is a watch with a second hand, a hill, and at least one coasting machine—like, say, the Buffy-Porson, for example.

For those of you who are new to the sport, a downhill race is just like a hill-climb race—such as the famous one at Pike's Peak, where champions battle it out in all sorts of powerful competition cars—only in reverse. You run against the clock *down* the hill instead of up.

There are all sorts of different styles of races that can be run on a downhill course. You can have simple Eliminations, with the driver who makes the length of the course in the shortest time emerging the winner. Or, you can write down all the times and add up the best five times for each driver (that way, you don't have to count your mistakes).

Or, if you happen to have two cars and two watches, you can run a "Hare and Hound" race by setting one car off five seconds before the next car; then time the distance between them at the finish line.

You can set up different kinds of starts, as well. With a "Le Mans"-style start, when the timer starts timing, he rings a bell (or any starting signal). Then the driver has to run from a starting line, jump into his car, and race to the finish. If you're short of starting officials and can't see the start from the finish line, then you can make a starting bell from a tin can with rocks in it. The driver can ring this from his cockpit just as he begins his run to start the timing.

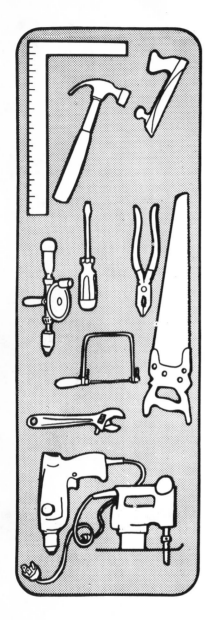

You don't need a whole workshop full of tools to build a Buffy-Porson. Ordinary, household hand tools will do the job.

One building aid that you *will* need once in a while is an Older Person to lend a hand when a special hole needs drilling or a tricky curve has to be cut.

If you think you're going to need a helper to cut a certain difficult curve, for instance, make sure you have the cut already marked with clear lines. And have all the tools you will need handy, with the lumber all ready to go *before* asking for a hand.

Don't forget that grownups often have very short attention spans (especially if there's a big game on TV). If they get the idea that you're asking them to do jobs that you could do just as well yourself, they tend to lose interest and their minds may wander. Keep their jobs simple, and they'll usually be a great help.

On the other hand, some grownups may tend to take over the whole project—which can be just as tricky. A gentle firmness on your part will usually remind them who is really running the show.

If you happen to have an older friend who has an electric drill and maybe an electric saber saw to use, then the job will go faster. But the Buffy-Porson can be built just as well with hand tools.

Making that first cut can be the hardest step of any project. And the question "where do I begin?!" can become quite a puzzle if you're not used to building things on your own.

Grownups often become discouraged at this point, and some even believe there's some sort of magic to building things that only "creative people" can figure out.

Sometimes it helps if you explain that any big project (like building a racer) isn't just one big mysterious puzzle that takes a "creative person" to solve. It's really just a bunch of small, simple jobs all grouped together to look bigger and more confusing than they really are—if you just take them one at a time.

When you finish the first step of the project, that makes the second step much easier to figure out. But if you stand back and try to figure out everything at one time, the whole project can look pretty confusing.

Just point out that if you take each step slowly, one at a time, you'll have the whole car built before you know it. And you'll find that there's nothing magic to building big things at all; just a lot of little simple jobs to be done one by one.

So, once you've gathered up enough materials to get under way, dive right into that first step, mark that first cut and start sawing before your helper has time to get confused. (You'll find a complete list of materials needed in the Appendix.)

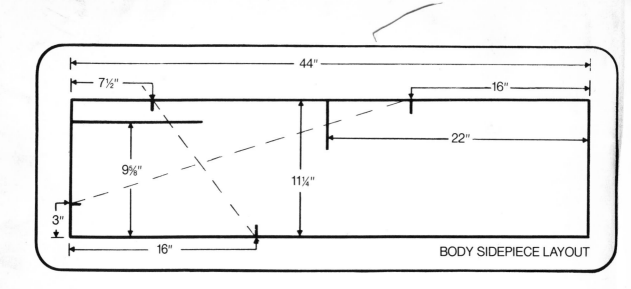

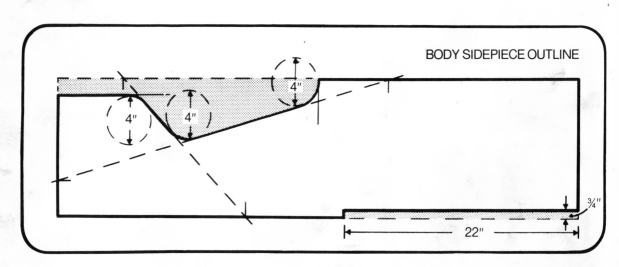

The first step is to draw the shape of the side of the car on one of the four-foot lengths of 1″ x 12″ board. Place the marks shown above around the edges of the board. Next, connect these marks with the straight lines shown below. Use a straight yardstick and a carpenter's square as a guide to draw the straight lines.

Once all the marks are sketched on lightly, connect the lines that form the outline shown at lower left with a heavier line. Then simply follow the heavy line when you actually cut out the piece a little later.

You can use a tin can that measures four inches across the bottom to draw the circles. It's best to mark all lines lightly at first.

Next, use the dimensions shown here to mark one of the frame rails onto a 1″ x 6″ board. Again, you can use a four-inch-wide can to mark the curves at one end.

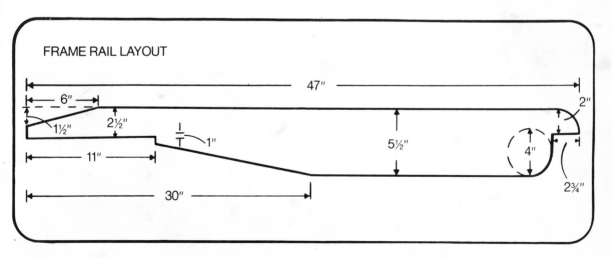

FRAME RAIL LAYOUT

47″

6″

1½″

2½″

2″

1″

5½″

4″

11″

30″

2¾″

Wherever possible, try to use a carpenter's crosscut saw to make the straight cuts. If you take a little extra time to make sure your cuts follow the lines, you'll save a lot of time later when you're fitting the parts together and smoothing them down. When you're cutting curves with the coping saw, the frame may sometimes get in the way. If this happens, just twist the handle loose, position the frame to one side out of the way, re-tighten the handle and saw on. The more firmly a board is held, the easier it will be to cut. So place the board on a firm, flat surface and get a helper to hold it down if it jumps around during cutting.

Once you've cut out one sidepiece and one frame rail, place each one on a similar piece of lumber and draw around the cut pieces onto the new lumber to mark matching pieces for the other side. Might as well cut these out, as long as they're marked.

Coping saws have a nasty habit of gradually slanting over to one side in the middle of a cut. To get around this, keep a steady eye on the blade to make sure it's not only following the line, but also cutting straight up and down.

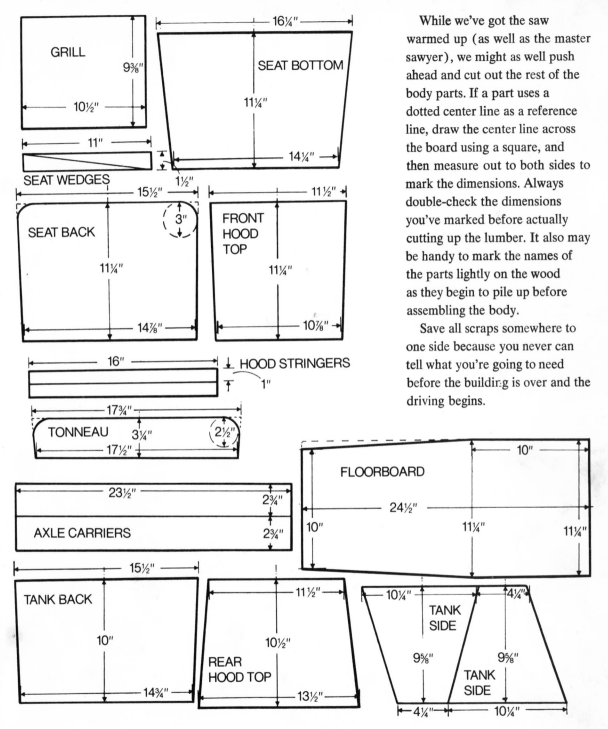

GRILL
9⅜"
10½"

16¼"
SEAT BOTTOM
11¼"
14¼"

11"
SEAT WEDGES
1½"

15½"
SEAT BACK
3"
11¼"
14⅞"

11½"
FRONT HOOD TOP
11¼"
10⅞"

16"
HOOD STRINGERS
1"

17¾"
TONNEAU
3¼"
2½"
17½"

23½"
AXLE CARRIERS
2¾"
2¾"

FLOORBOARD
10"
24½"
10"
11¼"
11¼"

15½"
TANK BACK
10"
14¾"

11½"
REAR HOOD TOP
10½"
13½"

10¼"
TANK SIDE
4¼"
9⅝"
9⅝"
TANK SIDE
4¼"
10¼"

While we've got the saw warmed up (as well as the master sawyer), we might as well push ahead and cut out the rest of the body parts. If a part uses a dotted center line as a reference line, draw the center line across the board using a square, and then measure out to both sides to mark the dimensions. Always double-check the dimensions you've marked before actually cutting up the lumber. It also may be handy to mark the names of the parts lightly on the wood as they begin to pile up before assembling the body.

Save all scraps somewhere to one side because you never can tell what you're going to need before the building is over and the driving begins.

15

T𝗐𝗈 Body Building

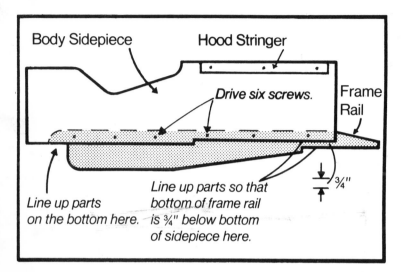

Body Sidepiece   Hood Stringer

Drive six screws.   Frame
Rail

*Line up parts so that
bottom of frame rail
is ¾" below bottom
of sidepiece here.*

*Line up parts
on the bottom here.*

¾"

Drill holes through the body sidepiece as marked with a ³⁄₁₆″ drill bit to guide the 1½″ screws into the frame rail. Remember that you'll want to put the frame rail on the right side of the right body sidepiece, and on the left side of the left body sidepiece. Mount the hood stringers to the sidepieces, flush at the top and on the inside of the car.

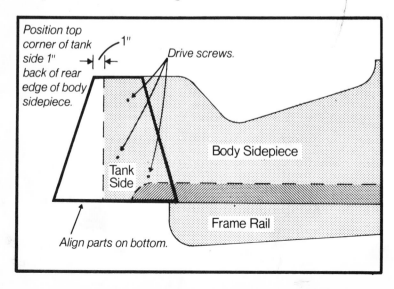

*Position top
corner of tank
side 1"
back of rear
edge of body
sidepiece.*

1"

Drive screws.

Body Sidepiece

Tank
Side

Frame Rail

Align parts on bottom.

The first step to putting the body together is to assemble the two sides, each of which is made up of the body sidepiece, the frame rail, the seat-tank brace and the hood stringer.

The positioning of these parts is pretty important, so it's a good idea to place them carefully on each other as shown here, and then draw around one part and onto the other (and vice versa) to mark the positions permanently.

Now a word about fasteners. A lot of people think that it's easier to put something together with nails than with screws because it's faster to drive in a nail than a screw. But for a machine that you don't want to come apart at the wrong time, screws are a better bet for a number of reasons.

First of all, it's hard to nail something like the Buffy-Porson together without knocking your first joint loose by the time you're nailing the last one together. Secondly, although screws hold things together much better than nails, they can be removed much more easily if you want to make an adjustment later on. Besides, don't let anybody kid you; nails these days are hard to drive!

Now you can screw the sidepieces to the frame rails, and the seat braces to the sidepieces.

Always spread plenty of white glue onto the joining surfaces whenever screwing two parts together (except when it is especially noted that glue shouldn't be used). The combination of glue and screws to clamp the joint tight will make a car that will take all sorts of beating.

It's a good idea to bear in mind how the parts will be used as you put them together. If it's a seat bottom, you're going to want to spend a little extra care to make doubly sure that the joints are strong.

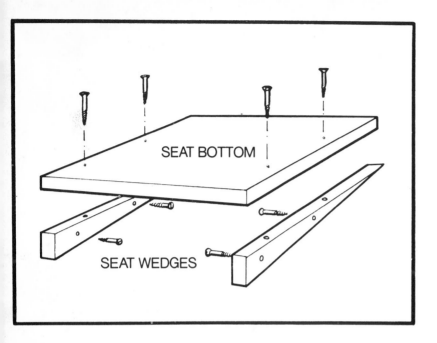

SEAT BOTTOM

SEAT WEDGES

Drill two ³⁄₁₆″ screw-guide holes through the sides of each seat wedge after it's mounted. Screws will extend through these, mounting the seat bottom to the insides of the frame rails.

Speaking of seat bottoms, we might as well assemble the one at hand. The wedge-shaped seat-bottom braces are to be positioned on the underside with the side ends of the wedges lined up (or "flush" as they say in the trade) with the front edge of the seat bottom. The outsides of the wedges should be flush with the side edges of the seat bottom. Drill two screw-guide holes down through the seat bottom, ³⁄₈″ in from the side edges, as shown, so that the screws will hit the centers of the wedges.

Next, add glue and drive the screws home, and you're ready to start the assembly shown at far right.

First, drill nine ³⁄₁₆″ screw-guide holes in the floorboard, as shown here. Then screw it up into position against the notch in the bottom of one sidepiece. Drill screw-guide holes through the frame rails in front of the grill position to fasten the frame rail to the edge of the floorboard piece at the front.

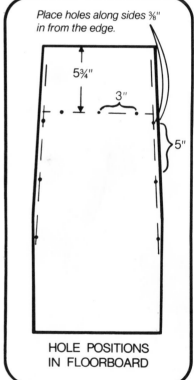

Place holes along sides ³⁄₈″ in from the edge.

5³⁄₄″

3″

5″

HOLE POSITIONS
IN FLOORBOARD

Next, drive screws up through the holes in the floorboard to fasten the bottom of the grill in place. Then drill ³⁄₁₆″ screw holes in through the body side, 3″ apart and ³⁄₈″ back from the vertical front line of the grill on the body sidepiece. Drive these screws in, fastening the body side to the grill piece.

Position the seat-bottom side edge against the inside of the frame rail. The bottom of the wedge should line up with the rail bottom, and the front of the wedge should be positioned where the rail bottom just begins to angle up toward the front. Mark this position on the frame and then drill holes so that the screws can extend in through the frame and into the side edge of the seat bottom. Now drive screws through the seat-bottom braces into the frame rail, and then more screws in through the holes in the rails and into the edge of the seat bottom.

Drill three holes to guide screws through the seat back and into the seat-back brace (³⁄₈″ in from the side edges of the seat back). Fasten the seat back against the brace, with the bottom edge of the seat back aligned with the bottom edge of the brace.

When the parts have been attached to one sidepiece, as above, spread glue on all the joining surfaces and attach the parts in the same order to the other side of the body, as below.

Drill a screw hole down through the tonneau piece at each corner, so that screws will extend down into the tops of the body sides behind the seat back. Then screw the tonneau piece in place. When this is in place go over the entire car with a damp rag to wipe away any glue drips. You may want to seal any gaps in the joints with a little extra glue spread into the joints to make painting a little easier later on.

Now that the first frantic wave of activity has died down
a little, the time has come to test out the cockpit (and col-
lect your wits a bit). You can afford, at this point, to sit
back, put your feet up, and congratulate yourself on having survived the hard part. You may even want to take the
opportunity to point out to your helper that the rest of the
project is all downhill from here—just a bunch of small
parts to be attached each in its turn.

Three
Getting Rolling

We can now begin to put the Buffy-Porson on its wheels. The first step is to fasten the back-axle carrier in place. Turn the body upside down and position the axle carrier in the notch at the back of the frame rail, sticking out an equal distance on both sides.

Then drill screw-guide holes down through the axle carriers so that two screws can be driven into the bottom of both sides of the car, fixing the carrier in place (with glue, of course).

The front-axle carrier is mounted by a ⁵⁄₁₆″-diameter (or larger) pivot bolt passing through the center of the carrier and on through the floorboard (at the center, one inch *in front* of the grill front).

With the car still upside down, mark the positions of these two holes and have your helper drill them if they prove to be a snag in the progress for you.

Spread a little grease or oil around the holes (on the car bottom and axle carrier top). Then insert the bolt through the hole, toward the bottom of the car. Slip two or three washers over the bolt. Then slip the top of the axle carrier over the bolt, slip on another washer, and two nuts. Tighten the first nut, then back it off a bit to allow the axle carrier to pivot. Finally, use two wrenches to tighten the second lock-nut down onto the first without tightening the first nut onto the carrier any more.

The axles are held onto the carriers with ½″ iron pipe straps (used in plumbing), bolted to the carriers. If the straps are a little large for the axle (as shown here), the axle can simply be wrapped in tape to make the fit snug and keep it from rattling. Slip a wheel over one end of the axle, with about ½″ extending beyond the outside of the wheel. Place the axle and wheel in position and then wrap the axle in tape just in from the ends of the axle carriers. Place the pipe straps over the taped axle about 1″ in from each end of the axle carrier.

Drill down through the holes in the straps and on through the axle carrier with a ¾₁₆″ drill bit. Next, drive the bolts up through the axle carriers and on through the holes in the pipe straps and tighten each down in place with a nut and lock-nut.

If you want to make a double-strength mounting for the axle, just to be on the safe side, place doubled-up pipe straps (one directly over the other) at each axle mounting and bolt through both straps.

Axle rods vary, and if yours seems a little flexible when you wiggle the free end of the axle, then you may want to add a third axle strap to the center of the back-axle carrier (which carries the bulk of the weight), as shown here.

Slip another wheel onto the longer end of both axles and mark a spot on the axle about ½″ outside the wheel where the axles should be cut off with a hacksaw. After cutting, place each end of both axles, one by one, up resting on something solid and make a dent in the axle about ¼″ in from the end with the hammer and a center punch. Then you may want to ask your helper to drill on through the axles at those points with a ⅛″ drill bit.

We're just about ready to mount the wheels, and they probably aren't even greased yet, right? If you have some axle grease handy, use that. Otherwise, motor oil will do. The clear, household machine oils are a little too thin for the rugged kind of bearings we're talking about. If your wheels don't happen to have bearings in them, then just apply the lubrication to the axle itself and hope for the best. They'll probably work fine as long as you keep them reasonably clean. (If it sounds like a pencil sharpener going when you spin the wheel, then it's time to clean the bearings in a little solvent, gas or kerosene, and then re-grease.)

To attach each wheel, slip a washer over the axle end, place the wheel on the axle, slip on a second washer, and then insert a cotter pin through the hole in the axle and bend it back so it can't fall out.

And there it is! Lo and behold, it's on its wheels.

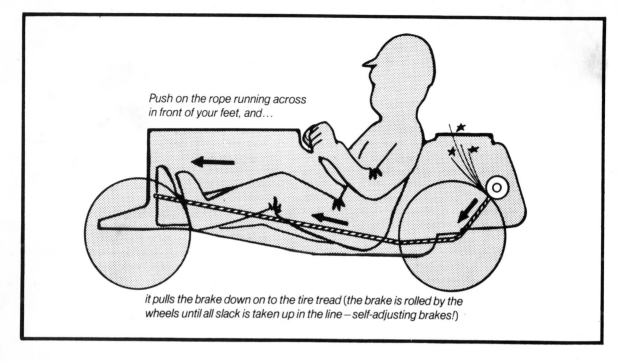

Push on the rope running across in front of your feet, and...

it pulls the brake down on to the tire tread (the brake is rolled by the wheels until all slack is taken up in the line — self-adjusting brakes!)

Now, before rigging the steering, we'd better turn our attention to the brakes—for obvious reasons. The brakes on the Buffy-Porson are simple, yet seem to be effective in all sorts of situations.

To stop the car, a rope runs across the car just in front of the driver's feet. From there it passes through an eye bolt on either side and back over the seat bottom, under the seat back, under the axle, and up to a 1″-diameter dowel hung on elastic bands. When the driver decides it's time to slow down, he pushes on the rope running across in front of him with his foot. This puts equal tension on both rope ends, bringing the dowel down onto the tires. The dowel is spun lightly by the tires, which increases the tension and automatically increases the pressure on the tires, bringing the whole show to a stop.

To rig the brakes, the first step is to drill two 1½″-diameter holes through the gas-tank sides with the centers of the holes 5″ down from the tops of the tank sides (for 14″ wheels). The holes can be drilled with a hole-saw attachment for power drills from the insides of the tank with the help of your crew.

The front of the holes should lie right up against the rear edges of the body sidepieces.

Next, cut the dowel to 28″ and wrap the ends with 2″-wide tape until the tape rests firmly against the tires when the dowel is pushed down and forward.

Now drive two short nails into the inner sides of the tank near the top, and tie two short loops of elastic around the dowel. Loop one end of each elastic over a nail to hold the dowel up off the tires at both ends. Finally, drill a ⁵⁄₁₆″ or ¼″ hole through both ends of the dowel just inside the tank sides.

Drill ¼″ holes for the eye bolts through the sides of the hood, 4″ from the top and 3″ or more behind the grill front (position these according to the height of the driver). Insert eye bolts from the inside, tighten down the nuts and cut off any excess bolt sticking out.

Insert one end of a ¼″-diameter braided nylon, dacron or polypropylene rope up through one hole in the dowel. Now thread the other end under the axle, over the seat bottom, through the eye bolts, and back down through the same route to the other hole in the dowel. Tie a knot in one end and then pull the rope until the brake is as tight against the wheel as you can get it; tie the knot in the other end.

The first few times that you press on the brakes the rope will stretch a good bit, freeing the wheels to turn. Keep tightening the adjustment by re-tying the knots for a while as needed until the rope runs out of stretch.

To apply more braking power in emergencies, simply pull up on the rope with one hand as you push on it with your foot.

The tank back is attached with screws running in through the tank sides and into the side edges of the tank back. Drill screw-guide holes through the sides and attach the tank back with screws, but do not glue. Then if you want to open the back to readjust the brakes, you can simply remove the top set of screws and tilt it back to see the works.

Whenever you're rigging up the controls, it's good to remember the sort of situations you'll be meeting in your Buffy-Porson— and take the extra time to make sure it's all solidly built. It also doesn't hurt to keep an eye on the rigging while you're using it. Things like ropes and bolts sometimes need re-tightening in the best of machines. And don't hesitate to replace a rope if it looks like it's becoming worn.

If the tape "brake shoes" begin to wear through after a while, you can either re-wrap them with more tape; or untie the ropes, rotate the brake dowel one-half turn, and then re-tie the ropes (with the unworn tape facing the tires).

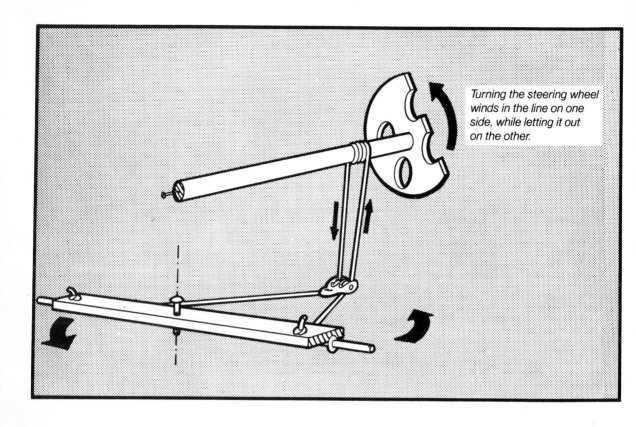

Turning the steering wheel winds in the line on one side, while letting it out on the other.

The layout of the steering system is probably already familiar to most of you. It's simply a version of the tried-and-true cable and bobbin steering used for years (even by some real racing cars in actual motor racing). The rope is tied to one end of the pivoted front axle, and from there runs back through one side of a double pulley, and up through a hole in the steering column. After wrapping around the column it heads back down through the other side of the pulley, and from there to the other end of the front axle.

32

The first step is to drill a hole near each end of the front-axle carrier. With a ¼″ or ⁵⁄₁₆″ drill bit, locate the holes about ½″ in front of the axle itself and about 1½″ in from the end of the axle carrier.

Insert one end of the rope (¼″-diameter braided nylon, dacron or polypropylene) up through the hole near the right front wheel and then tie a knot in it and lead the other end back.

Turn the car over and mount a 4″ x 3″ scrap from the leftover lumber and the bottom of the floorboard piece with screws and glue. The 3″ side of the block should be aligned with the rear edge of the floorboard.

Now, position a double pulley along the center line of the car with the pulley wheels facing the rear and the mounting eye facing the front of the car. Align the axle of the pulley wheels with the rear edge of the floorboard and mark the position of the mounting eye on the scrap piece. Drill a ⁵⁄₁₆″ hole through the boards at this point and mount the pulley in position with a ⁵⁄₁₆″ bolt. Tighten the bolt until the pulley sinks into the wood block firmly and then run on a lock-nut.

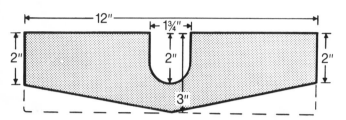

DASHBOARD

|← 12" →|
|← 1¾" →|
2"   2"   2"
3"

First, sketch in a 3" x 12" rectangle, draw a center line across it, and then draw in the angles and curve to be cut.

Cut the dashboard shown at left from a scrap of lumber and then mount this between the body sides, flush at the top edge with the sidepieces.

Drive mounting screws in through the dashboard and into the ends of the hood-mounted stringers and then drill starter holes and drive screws in through both body sidepieces and into the ends of the dash.

We used a length of 1⅝" -diameter dowel (the kind used in closets to hang clothes on) for a steering column. Try not to substitute anything much smaller than this because it will upset the steering ratio. Cut the column to a length of 22" and then drill a ⅛" hole in the center of one end and then a ³⁄₁₆" hole through the grill front, 1¼" down from the top, and in the center. Countersink this hole and then drive a screw through the hole and into the end of the column. Now loosen the screw about ½" turn so that the column (and screw) can turn freely in the grill hole.

Oil the front of the column and the column rest in the dashboard. Next, drill a ⁵⁄₁₆" or ¼" hole through the steering column, 4" forward of its rear end.

To rig the steering, set the front wheels pointing as far as they can to the left. Run the rope back from the tied end at the right end of the axle, under the floorboard, through the right side of the double block pulley, and then up through the hole in the column. Brace the front wheels still to the left, take up the slack and drive a small nail through the column to lock the rope in place in the hole.

Now, lead the free end of the rope over the steering column and down to the *right* side of the column, under the column and up and over again for a total of three turns around the column.

Next, lead the free end down through the left side of the double block and up to the hole through the left end of the axle carrier. Thread the rope up through this hole, pull up the slack in the rope and tie a knot. You'll want to re-tie this knot to tighten the steering rope as it stretches at first.

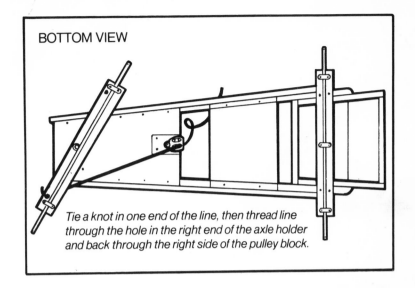

BOTTOM VIEW

Tie a knot in one end of the line, then thread line through the hole in the right end of the axle holder and back through the right side of the pulley block.

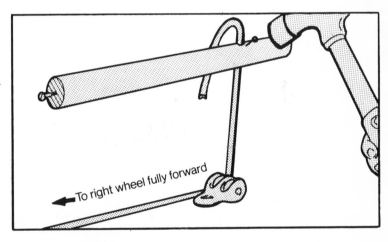

To right wheel fully forward

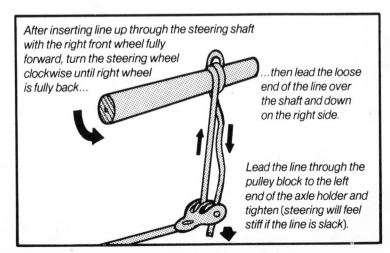

After inserting line up through the steering shaft with the right front wheel fully forward, turn the steering wheel clockwise until right wheel is fully back...

...then lead the loose end of the line over the shaft and down on the right side.

Lead the line through the pulley block to the left end of the axle holder and tighten (steering will feel stiff if the line is slack).

To make the steering wheel, we'll need a scrap of plywood about 10″ square and at least ½″ thick. To draw a circle for the wheel, drill two starter holes through a stick, 4½″ apart. Insert a nail or screw through one hole, a pencil into the other, push the screw or nail down onto the center of the plywood, and then simply draw around in a circle with the pencil.

Next, draw a line through the center of the circle, and then another line across this one, using a square. Place marks across these lines about 2″ in from the circle. To cut out the wheel, get your crew to drill four 2″ to 2½″ holes through at these marks with a hole-saw attachment for the power drill. Next, cut out the outline of the wheel with a coping saw. Drill a $\frac{5}{16}$″ hole through the center of the wheel, and then cut across the centers of two of the hole cut-outs so that you can get in and out of the car with maximum ease.

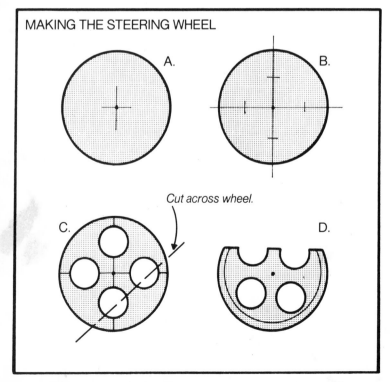

MAKING THE STEERING WHEEL

A.

B.

Cut across wheel.

C.

D.

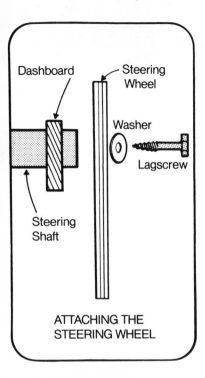

Dashboard

Steering
Wheel

Washer

Lagscrew

Steering
Shaft

ATTACHING THE
STEERING WHEEL

The wheel is held in place on the steering shaft with a 3″ x ⁵⁄₁₆″ lag screw (a large screw with a bolt head on the end of it). Drill a ¼″ starter hole straight into the center of the end of the steering column.

To attach the wheel, slip a wide washer over the lag screw, insert the lag screw through the center hole in the steering wheel, and then into the center hole of the steering column. Spread some glue on the end of the steering column, grip the column with one hand, and then tighten down on the lag screw with a wrench until the wheel is firmly mounted. You may need a little extra muscle to do this, so call on your large partner, if need be.

To keep the wheel from loosening at the wrong moment, we put in a safety screw on either side of the lag screw. Angle the starter holes in toward the center of the steering shaft slightly to keep the shaft from splitting. After checking to make certain the steering system is working, attach the hood tops by running screws at each corner of both boards down onto the hood stringer strips just inside the body sidepieces (and not down into the sidepieces, because you'll want to round off this corner before painting).

Don't use glue when mounting the hood pieces, just in case you need to get at the steering system or brakes at some future date.

The time has come, at last, to put the Buffy-Porson through its first grueling road tests. After a pre-test check of the brakes and steering rigging, take the Buffy-Porson to an easy, gradual slope, with plenty of open space—some quiet place away from crowds and distractions. And then put the Buffy through its paces.

After cornering and braking hard a number of times on an easy slope, check over all the ropes, all the pivot bolts, axle mounts, knots, wheels, steering mounts, and pulleys carefully. If anything shows signs of pulling loose, now is the time to put it right.

Once the car has passed its road tests to your satisfaction, you can start the process of finishing and painting. Rounding off a few corners can make a tremendous difference in the appearance of the car. And you may want to explain to your helper that any extra effort put into the smoothing will be paid back every time you catch a glimpse of the glossy smoothness of the flawless bodywork in years to come.

Rounding corners is done better with a serrated wood shaper than with the old-style wood plane. They're easier to work with and do the job faster, as well. If you want to speed the process up a bit, get your partner to run a drum-type serrated shaper attachment on his power drill to round off the corners.

To shape your Buffy-Porson like the one shown here, you'll want to round off some corners and leave others fairly sharp. Round off the top side edges of the hood, the top of the seat back, the top and bottom edges of the gas tank, the top edge around the tonneau piece, and the vertical rear end edges of the body sides; also the tops of the cockpit edges.

You'll want to leave the following corners fairly sharp: the frame rails, the axle carriers, the edges around the grill front, the side edges of the gas tank, and the seat bottom. Might as well round off the edge around the steering wheel so that it feels good to grip, while we're at it.

Before sanding, use the crosscut saw to cut lines marking the front and rear edges of the hood. Use a square to mark the lines up the sides of the hood at the positions shown at right. Connect these lines over the top of the hood and then cut down into the hood along these lines about ⅛″ deep.

Cut a hood hinge strap from ½″ half-round molding to fit between the two hood lines with the strip sitting down the center of the hood. For a little added realism you can cut shallow notches over the top of the strip every 2″ or so. Glue and nail the strip in place with short brads before sanding the car.

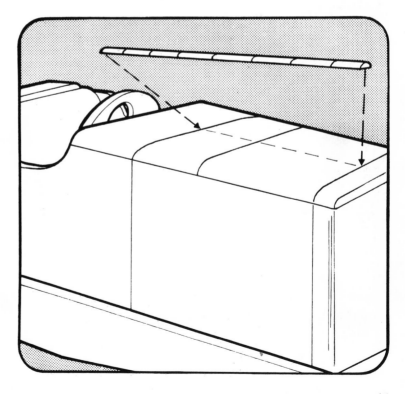

Sand the car with coarse sandpaper along the rounded-off corners to remove any lumps left by the shaper. Next, sand the entire car with medium and then fine sandpaper to remove any scratches left by the coarse paper. If you wrap the sandpaper around a small, flat block of wood, it will help you smooth down the high spots in a hurry.

Now a word or two about painting: some people say that a coat of paint will hide a thousand mistakes—and it can. But if you're a little sloppy about it, a coat of paint can *add* a thousand more mistakes that will stand out like a sore thumb. The key to painting success depends on two things: going slowly and carefully (keeping a close eye on your work); and using lots of thin coats rather than trying to get by with one or two heavy coats.

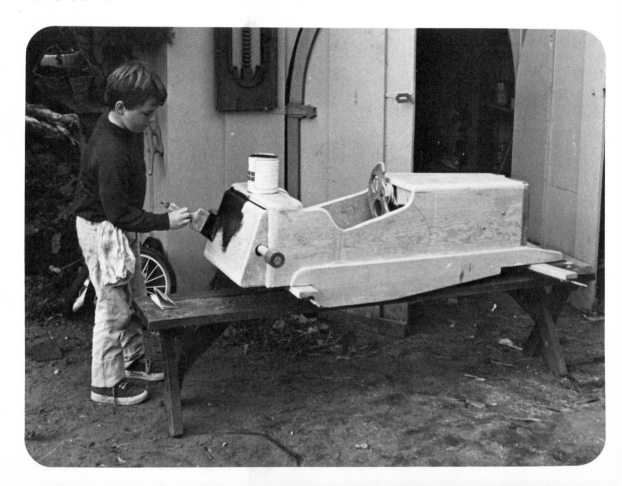

By "thin coats" we don't mean thinning the paint way down, but rather keeping the thickness of the actual coat from getting too heavy, resulting in drips. Once you've spread the paint on, covering an area, don't stop there. Keep on stroking the area with your brush to *remove* any excess paint that may turn into a drip. Don't try to make it look like the finished product in one coat (no matter what it says on the paint can), and let each coat dry thoroughly before adding the next (or the paint may curdle up like a relief map of the moon before your very eyes —a calamity that results in much extra sanding time). Any good-quality gloss enamel should do the job nicely on the body. You might want to use a flat-finish enamel on the seat and interior for contrast. But stay away from old paint that has been sitting around a long time—it can cause a lot of problems.

Four
Testing and Finishing

A lot of the fun of a car like the Buffy-Porson comes from all the little parts and accessories hung all over it: the hood strap, the exhaust pipe, the spare wheel and such.

Of course, none of these bits and pieces is strictly needed, so you don't really have to put any of them on if you don't feel like it. And maybe that's why they're so much fun to add — you can put them on just about any way you please, and any time you get around to it. You can start using the car as soon as you can steer and stop it. Put the accessories on as you find them, adding to the Buffy as time goes on.

No race car such as the Buffy-Porson is complete without at least one hood strap. Any old belt with a slight curve in it (when laid out flat) will do. Just place the buckle a little to one side on the top of the hood, and run the belt down the side to the top of the frame rail. Cut the belt in two at this point, buckle the two ends together, drape it over the hood, covering the crack between the hood top pieces, and attach the cut belt ends to the hood sides with short screws or round-head upholstery tacks.

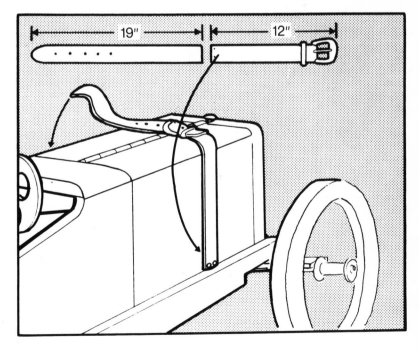

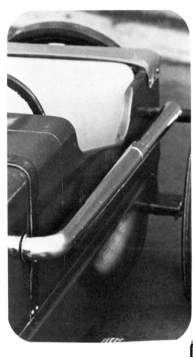

Old plumbing drain elbows from under a defunct sink can make a handsome exhaust set up (and they're not too expensive brand new, if you find that people object to having their sinks tampered with).

With a hole-cutting attachment, cut from a scrap of wood a round plug that will fit just inside the bent end of the pipe in question. Screw this plug to the left side of the hood about halfway down, just in front of the hood belt. Slip the end of the pipe over the plug, drill a hole through the end and screw the pipe to the plug.

Drill a hole through the pipe near the back end for a long mounting screw to extend through the pipe, then through a 1″-long piece of garden hose, and into the side of the body.

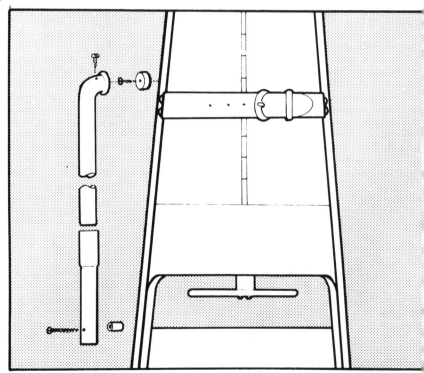

Paint the radiator shell in front of the hood line with silver aluminum-finish paint. A couple of coats will deepen the gloss a little. Then use the pattern included in the Appendix to trace two patterns for the opposite sides of the "grill opening" and cut out these shapes from black Contact paper, which is then peeled from its backing and stuck in place over the aluminum paint.

To make a professional-looking number, draw a 7½"-diameter circle onto white Contact paper, using a plate as a guide. Then cut your favorite number out of black Contact paper and stick the white and then black paper down in position.

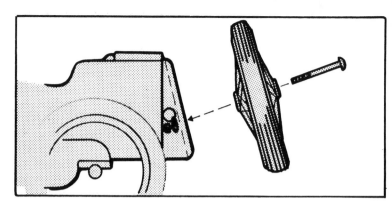

To mount the spare wheel, draw a center line down the back of the gas tank and mark a spot for a ⅜″ hole, 6″ down from the top of the tank. Insert a 4″-long, ⁵⁄₁₆″ round-head bolt through the wheel hub, through the tank, and then tighten firmly.

A standard bicycle squeeze-horn mounts nicely to the side of the hood, just forward of the cockpit. For most mounts, drill two holes through the side of the body (you may need to drill a second bolt hole if the mount has only one). Then extend the screws or bolts out through the holes and into the mount.

To cover the tonneau, drape a piece of fabric or leatherette (about 7″ x 20″) that you like over the tonneau piece and then tack down the sides with round-head upholstery tacks, tuck the front edge down behind the seat back, tuck the back edge down in front of the tank back, and trim off the sides below the tacks. If you can't find a piece of material that strikes your fancy, paint the tonneau with a flat-finish paint of a contrasting color and drive the tacks in around the edges anyway.

The radiator cap can be made from a jar cap, hose cap or a round wood drawer-pull painted silver. Drill a small hole in the center and nail the cap in place on top of the grill.

To make a dashboard with the proper spirit, first varnish or stain the dashboard piece. Then you can add "instrument dials" by painting in circles of a contrasting color, by nailing small jar caps in place, or by cutting out circles from white Contact paper and sticking them on in place, as shown below. You can always drive in small finishing nails at the base of each dial and then bend them over for dial needles.

Sooner or later, of course, the work will come to a halt. And after a lot of effort, some fun and some problems, a gleaming new Buffy-Porson stands ready for its first public appearance.

At this stage, the car stops being a project and starts being a sporting proposition: something that will give you a chance to do things you couldn't do before. It's only a matter of time now before you will be charging off down the hill together—and a lot depends on both of you.

It seems like a long time since the Buffy-Porson was just a pile of lumber and hardware. And if you've gotten this far, you probably know that you've both changed a bit since the first few steps of the project.

Time now for some well-earned fun. And while we're at it, a few safety precautions never hurt. A helmet and a set of unbreakable goggles or glasses can make you feel better about a lot of things.

The time has come to put it on the line (the starting line, in this case), and either make a great fool of yourself right in front of everybody—or to take the risk, and come out smiling. It's time to get on with the festivities and see what a Buffy-Porson's really made of.

Things look a little different from behind the wheel! And some corners seem to have a way of sneaking up on you before you know it!

Through one corner. Now through another. Hey, this isn't so scary. In fact, it's fun!

Yipes. Better not start getting cocky. Even a Buffy-Porson won't steer itself!

Made it! After the first run, you begin to get an idea of what downhill driving really is. Just wait till the next run! (And it seems like you always seem to have enough energy and time left for "just one more run.")

That's our story, and we're sticking to it.

Appendix

Materials List

Lumber:

- 2 4-foot, 1"x6" pine or fir stock (or 1 8-footer)
- 6 4-foot, 1"x12" pine or fir stock (or 3 8-footers)
- 1 18", ½"-wide half-round molding
- 1 24", 1⅝"-diameter softwood dowel
- 1 36", 1"-diameter hardwood dowel
- 1 10"x10" scrap of ½"- to ¾"-thick plywood

Fasteners:

- 100 1½"-long, #8 flat-head plated wood screws
- 1 2½"-long, ⁵⁄₁₆"-diameter lag screw
- 10 1½"-long, ³⁄₁₆"-diameter machine bolts and 20 nuts
- 2 2½"-long, ⁵⁄₁₆"-diameter carriage bolts and nuts
- 2 2"-long, ¼"-diameter eye bolts and nuts
- 1 4"-long, ⁵⁄₁₆"-diameter carriage bolt and two nuts
- 12 Washers for ½" bolts

Hardware:

- 5 14"-overall-diameter spoke wheels and tires
- 5 ½" iron pipe straps (10 if using doubled straps)
- 2 36"-long iron rods (⁷⁄₁₆"- or ½"-diameter; check to fit wheels)
- 4 Cotter pins
- 1 Galvanized double pulley block (about 2½" long)
- 20 Feet of ¼"-diameter braided nylon, dacron or polypropylene rope
- 20 Inches of elastic strap
- 1 Roll of 2"-wide gray tape

After painting, trace this grill shape to make a pattern. Then use the pattern to draw a left and a right side of the grill onto black Contact paper. Cut the sides out and stick in place on the grill front.

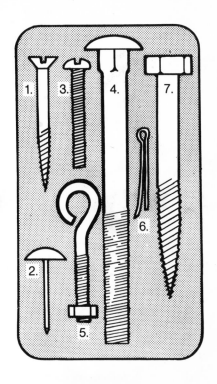

What it all looks like:

1. 1½″, #8 flat-head wood screw; 2. round-head up-holstery tack; 3. machine bolt; 4. carriage bolt; 5. eye bolt; 6. cotter pin; 7. lag screw;

a. double pulley block; b. pipe strap; c. braided line; d. half-round molding.

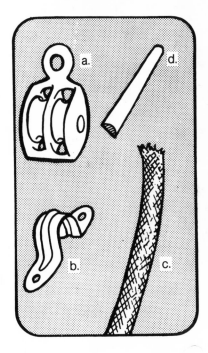